Dessert Designer

DESIGNING CREATIVE COOKIES

SMART COOKIE

by Dana Meachen Rau

CAPSTONE PRESS
a capstone imprint

Snap Books are published by Capstone Press,
1710 Roe Crest Drive, North Mankato, Minnesota 56003.
www.capstonepub.com

Library of Congress Cataloging-in-Publication Data
Rau, Dana Meachen, 1971–
Smart cookie : designing creative cookies / by Dana Meachen Rau.
p. cm.—(Snap books. Dessert designer)
Includes bibliographical references and index.
Summary: "Step-by-step instructions teach readers how to create
food art with cookies"—Provided by publisher.
ISBN 978-1-4296-8619-8 (library binding)
ISBN 978-1-62065-342-5 (ebook pdf)
1. Cookies—Juvenile literature. 2. Cake decorating—Juvenile
literature. I. Title.
TX772.R383 2013
641.86'539—dc23

2011052722

Editor: Jennifer Besel
Designer: Juliette Peters
Food and Photo Stylist: Brent Bentrott
Prop Preparation: Sarah Schuette
Scheduler: Marcy Morin
Production Specialist: Kathy McColley

Photo Credits:
All photos by Capstone Studio/Karon Dubke
    except:
Tania McNaboe, p. 32 (author's photo)

Printed in the United States of America in
North Mankato, Minnesota.
042012   006682CGF12

table of contents

THINK OUTSIDE the JAR

What can you make with cookies, candy, and a little icing? Anything you want! Cookies from the jar are yummy. But you can upgrade them to extreme coolness by adding another ingredient—your imagination. Almost anything you can dream up, you can create on a cookie.

How to Use This Book

Follow the simple steps for each project to make some extremely cool cookies. Remember to always check with an adult if you are using a knife, the microwave, or other kitchen tools and appliances.

Once you get decorating, there'll be no stopping you! But you do need to learn one very important skill first. For all the projects in this book, you need to know how to make royal icing.

Royal icing hardens into a firm shell so your cookies have a smooth finish. It also holds decorations and glues cookies together. There are two kinds of royal icing. Flood royal icing is thinner and good for filling in large areas. Edge icing is thicker and good for making details and edges.

ROYAL ICING

Edge Icing

2 teaspoons (10 mL) meringue powder *
2 tablespoons (30 mL) water
2 to 2½ cups (480 to 600 mL)
    confectioner's sugar

With a mixer on high, blend the
ingredients together in a bowl for about
four to five minutes. The icing is the
right consistency when it forms little
peaks that hold their shape.

Makes 1 cup of icing

Flood Icing

Make a batch of edge icing. Then add
water ½ teaspoon (2.5 mL) at a time,
blending after each addition. The icing
is ready when drips hold their shape for
just a moment before they blend back
into the icing.

Keep royal icing in airtight containers
when you're not using it. If you don't, a
crust will start to form on the top. You
can keep icing for about a week at room
temperature. Rewhip before you use it.

* You can find meringue powder in the
cake decorating sections of hobby and
craft stores.

DECORATOR'S TOOLBOX

A painter needs brushes and canvases. A carpenter needs hammers and nails. A cookie decorator like you needs tools too!

~ wax paper ~
Use this supply to keep taffy and other sticky stuff from sticking to your workspace.

~ piping bag ~
This fabric or plastic bag holds frosting and is used to decorate anything from cookies to cakes.

~ kitchen shears ~
These scissors are designed for use with food.

~ rolling pin ~
This is a handy tool for flattening taffies.

~ cooling rack ~
Not only is this tool good for cooling goodies, but the slats let icing drip off a project for a smooth finish.

~ food coloring ~
Food coloring makes your icing stand out. Just put a drop of liquid or a dab of gel into your icing. You'll find a little goes a long way.

~ bowls ~
Keep a variety of these around to mix up icing.

~ tweezers ~
Use tweezers to place those tiny decorations in just the right place.

~ decorating tips ~
These go on the piping bag to create cool designs with icing.

~ cookie cutters ~
These are great for forming cookie dough into shapes. But you can also use them to cut already baked round sugar cookies into shapes too!

~ cutting board ~
Do any cutting on the cutting board to avoid damaging kitchen counters.

~ sharp knife ~
You need this to cut cookies or decorations.

~ toothpicks ~
These are great for spreading the flood icing over your cookies.

~ spoons ~
Have a bunch of spoons ready to stir up a rainbow of icing colors.

~ zip-top bags ~
These make great substitutes for piping bags.

CLEAR SKY
RAINBOWS

After a thunderstorm the skies clear, and nature treats you to an amazing colorful display. Bring a rainbow into the kitchen with a 3-D display of your own.

INGREDIENTS

edge icing
red, orange, yellow, green, blue,
   and purple food coloring
2 large round sugar cookies
flood icing
1 chocolate covered caramel
10 pieces yellow candy buttons

Tip:
Experiment with piping tips to get the look you want when decorating with icing. Round tips are great for outlining details. Basket weave tips can make long, ribbed stripes.

If using a zip-top plastic bag, experiment with how you snip the tip of the bag. Cut it small for detailed decorations or wide to cover large areas.

1. Divide the edge icing into eight bowls. Keep one bowl white. Tint six of the bowls into the colors of the rainbow. Tint the last bowl a light blue. Place the icings into eight piping bags.

2. Cut one cookie in half. On one half, use white icing to pipe half a cloud shape in the right-hand corner. With the red icing, pipe an arch along the outer edge of the cookie to meet the cloud. Repeat with the orange, yellow, green, blue, and purple.

3. Divide the flood icing into two bowls. Keep one bowl white. Tint the other light blue.

4. Spoon white flood icing into the cloud shape. Then spoon blue flood icing into the small arch under your rainbow. Use a toothpick to spread the icing. Set the cookie aside for about 30 minutes until the icing hardens.

5. Next, pipe a ring of light blue edge icing around the outer edge of the full cookie. Pipe a cloud shape on the right side with the white edge icing. Spoon white flood icing into the cloud shape and blue flood icing onto the rest of the cookie.

6. While the flood icing is still wet, place the rainbow upright on top. Match up the clouds on both cookies.

7. Cover the bottom of a chocolate covered caramel with yellow edge icing. Stick the candy buttons to the icing to look like gold coins. Place your pot of gold at the end of the rainbow.

8. Let the cookie sit for a few hours to completely harden.

Makes 1 rainbow

WISE OLD OWL

You're one smart cookie. So are owls. These
wise birds won't help you with your homework.
But they know a lot about being delicious!

INGREDIENTS
edge icing
purple, blue, and brown
   food coloring
1 large round sugar cookie
flood icing
2 white candy wafers
1 orange jelly bean
yellow fruit leather

1. Divide the edge icing into three
small bowls. Add purple food coloring
to one, blue to another, and leave the
third white.

2. With the purple edge icing, pipe a
half-circle shape onto the top half of the
cookie. Pipe triangles down each side.

3. With the blue icing, complete the
circle by piping a line to connect
the bottoms of the two triangles.

4. Mix up a batch of flood icing. Divide it
into two bowls. Add purple to one bowl
and blue to the other to match the edge
icing colors.

5. Spoon the purple flood icing into the
purple triangles and half circle. Spoon
the blue flood icing into the middle area.
Spread the icings with toothpicks to fill in
the areas completely.

6. Pipe horizontal lines with the white
edge icing across the blue area. With a
toothpick, drag lines through the blue icing
from bottom to top, and then back down
again. This will make white feather shapes.

7. Place the wafer candies and orange jelly
bean onto the cookie to make the owl's face.
Color a bit of white edge icing brown. Pipe
two brown icing dots for eyes.

8. Cut a small triangle from the fruit
leather. Snip one edge to look like feathers.
Round the corner opposite the feather
snips, and carefully fit the leather between
the eyes.

9. Let the cookie sit for a few hours to
completely harden.

Makes 1 owl

Tip:
Dragging a toothpick through lines of
icing can create some cool effects, such
as feathers, tie-dye, or fireworks.

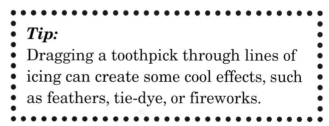

FANCY TOPPER

Ready to create a red carpet showstopper that's good enough to eat? Hats off to this glamorous project.

INGREDIENTS
chocolate melting wafers
pink food coloring
edge icing
flood icing
1 large round sugar cookie
1 vanilla sandwich cookie
buttercream frosting

1. Place five melting wafers in a small zip-top bag. Leave the bag open and microwave on the defrost setting for 30 seconds. Squeeze the melted candy to one corner. If the wafers are not soft yet, microwave on defrost 30 seconds more. With a kitchen shears, snip off the corner of the bag.

2. On a piece of wax paper, pipe the melted chocolate into shapes that will decorate your hat. Let them dry for at least one hour.

3. Mix up batches of pink edge and flood icings. Pipe a blob of edge icing into the middle of the large cookie. Place the sandwich cookie on top.

4. Pipe a ring of edge icing around the outer edge of the bottom cookie.

5. Spoon the flood icing on top of the sandwich cookie. It will pour over the sides and down onto the bottom cookie. Spread with a toothpick to cover all areas.

6. While the icing is wet, place your chocolate decorations against the top cookie.

7. Let the cookie hat sit for a few hours to completely harden.

8. Pipe more melted chocolate around the bottom of the small cookie. If you wish, use buttercream frosting to add frosting flowers or other decorations to the hat.

Makes 1 hat

Tip:
Melting wafers are solid candy circles that can be melted easily. The melted candy can be used for dipping or molding into new shapes. Each package has directions, so be sure to follow them carefully.

PUDDLE WITCH

When the wicked witch melted, who knew she would leave so much sweetness behind?

INGREDIENTS
green food coloring
edge icing
1 large round sugar cookie
flood icing
1 flat, round chocolate cookie
1 mini peanut butter cup
chocolate frosting
1 chocolate kiss
1 piece yellow taffy
1 pretzel stick
1 chocolate chew

~ shaping Taffy ~
You can soften taffy by warming it two ways. One way is by squeezing the taffy between your fingers and in your hands. Or you can place the taffy in the microwave for about five seconds. Once the taffy is warm, flatten, roll, cut, or mold it into any shape you want. Be sure to cover your work surface with wax paper so the taffy won't stick.

1. Add green food coloring to the edge icing.

2. Pipe a ring of green edge icing around the cookie. Make it wavy like a puddle.

3. Tint the flood icing green to match your edge icing. Spoon the flood icing onto the cookie and spread with a toothpick to cover all areas.

4. For the hat, place the chocolate cookie on top of the green puddle. Glue the peanut butter cup to the flat cookie with a small blob of chocolate frosting. Use a dab of chocolate frosting to stick the kiss to the peanut butter cup.

5. For the broom, place the taffy between two pieces of wax paper. Roll it flat with a rolling pin. Then cut it into thin strips. Mold these strips onto one end of the pretzel stick. Pinch and roll a small piece of chocolate chew into a thin strip. Wrap the strip around the taffy and pretzel. Trim the ends of the yellow strips to the same length. Place the broom on the green puddle.

6. Let the cookie sit for a few hours to completely harden.

Makes 1 witch cookie

Want another idea to go with this witch?
Add a little spider that sits down beside her!

INGREDIENTS
edge icing
black food coloring
orange or purple round fruit candy

Mix up a batch of black edge icing. Place the fruit candy on a piece
of wax paper. Pipe eight icing legs from the top of the candy to the
wax paper. Let the spider sit for a few hours to completely harden.
Then place your spider on the cookie's green puddle before it dries.

IN THE
Doghouse

Warm your heart with this sweet treat. Pet lovers will adore this playful twist on a gingerbread house.

INGREDIENTS

edge icing
9 square graham crackers
blue food coloring
1 large marshmallow
1 small gingersnap cookie
flood icing
1 brown jelly bean
2 mini chocolate chips
1 chocolate chew
1 red round fruit candy
1 sour candy strip

1. Place most of the edge icing in a piping bag. Leave a small amount in a bowl. Pipe this white icing around the sides of one graham cracker. Place the cracker flat on a piece of wax paper.

2. Pipe around all four sides of the next graham cracker, and glue it upright to one side of the base. Repeat with the other three sides, gently squeezing them together.

3. Cut one of the graham cracker squares in half to form two triangles. Edge each with icing and place one on top of the front "wall" and one on the back wall.

4. Pipe around the last two crackers and place them on the triangles to make a roof.

5. Let the doghouse sit for 15 minutes. Then pipe edge icing on the roof to make icicles.

6. Tint the bowl of icing with blue food coloring. Put in a piping bag.

7. Cut the last cracker into fourths. Pipe your puppy's name on one of the cracker pieces. Glue the name tag to the roof with white icing. Set the house aside to harden for about an hour.

8. To make your puppy, cut the large marshmallow in half. Use edge icing to glue a marshmallow half onto the cookie as a snout.

9. Spoon white flood icing over the marshmallow and cookie. Stick on the jelly bean as a nose and the two chocolate chips for eyes.

10. Warm the chocolate chew in the microwave for five seconds. Place it between two pieces of wax paper and roll it flat with a rolling pin. Cut two ear shapes from the candy, and place them on the dog's head.

11. Place a red fruit candy on the side of the snout for a tongue.

12. Let your puppy harden for about an hour. Then glue him on the front of the doghouse with some edge frosting.

13. Cut the sour candy strip into a hat shape. Glue it onto the dog's head with a little icing. Trim the ends of the candy strip to look like a scarf. Tuck these under his neck with a little edge frosting.

Makes 1 house and dog

Tip:
In this project, the icing in the piping bag will sit between uses. The icing may harden and clog up the tip. To prevent this, wet a paper towel and put it in the bottom of a glass. Place your piping bag in the glass so the tip sits on the wet towel.

BUgging OUT

Buzz around the kitchen to make these bee-utiful bugs. Finally some bugs people want at their picnic!

INGREDIENTS
edge icing
red and yellow food coloring
flood icing
1 black licorice whip
2 chocolate sandwich cookies
flood icing
8 mini chocolate chips
2 chocolate sprinkles
2 pale yellow candy wafers

1. Divide the edge icing into three small bowls. Add red food coloring to one and yellow food coloring to another. Keep the third bowl white.

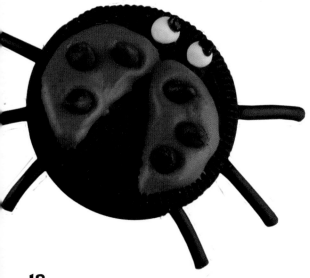

2. Divide the flood icing into two small bowls. Add red food coloring to one bowl and yellow to the other to match the edge icing.

3. Cut six small pieces of licorice whip for the legs. Open the top of one sandwich cookie. Pipe three dots of white edge icing along each side to hold the six legs. Squeeze a blob of icing in the middle of the cookie and glue the top back on.

4. With the red edge icing, pipe the shape of two red wings on top of the cookie. Spoon the red flood icing into the wing areas. Spread it with a toothpick to cover well.

5. While the icing is still wet, add six mini chocolate chips as spots. With the white edge icing, pipe two small eyes. Stick chocolate sprinkles in for eyeballs.

6. Cut a small piece of licorice whip for the bee's stinger. Open the top of the other sandwich cookie. Pipe a dot of white edge icing on the bottom and glue on the stinger.

7. Pipe lines of edge icing on each side of the inside of the cookie. Place one candy wafer on each side as wings. Squeeze a blob of icing in the middle of the cookie and glue the top back on.

8. Pipe three bands of yellow edge icing on top of the cookie. Spoon yellow flood icing into the bands and cover well.

9. While the icing is still wet, add two mini chocolate chips as eyes.

10. Let the cookies sit for a few hours to completely harden.

Makes 1 bee and 1 ladybug

FAIRY RING

Legend says that rings of mushrooms grow where fairies danced. Coax the shy little sprites out of hiding for a magical party of your own.

INGREDIENTS
flood icing
red food coloring
brown food coloring
5 vanilla wafer cookies
3 oatmeal cookies
edge icing
5 large marshmallows
5 chocolate chews
pink, green, and yellow taffy

1. Divide the flood icing into two bowls. Add red food coloring to one. Tint the other bowl light brown.

2. Place the vanilla wafers on a cooling rack, with a piece of wax paper below them. Spoon red flood icing over each cookie so it completely covers them. Let them sit for about an hour.

3. Stack the oatmeal cookies together with a spoonful of brown flood icing between each later. Completely cover the top cookie with brown flood icing. Set aside to harden for about an hour.

4. Divide the edge icing into two small bowls. Make one bowl dark brown. Keep the other bowl white. Place the icing into piping bags.

5. With the white edge icing, pipe dots on the top of a red cookie. Then pipe a blob of icing on the bottom of it. Place the cookie on top of a marshmallow. Repeat with the other cookies and marshmallows.

6. Warm the chocolate chews between two pieces of wax paper in the microwave for about five seconds. Roll them flat with a rolling pin.

7. Mold the chews onto the outside of the cookie stack to look like bark.

8. With the brown edge icing, pipe circles on the stump to look like tree rings.

9. With the white edge icing, pipe fairy wings on a piece of wax paper. Set aside to harden for about two hours.

10. Warm the pink taffy in the microwave. Roll a small round ball for the head and longer pieces for arms, legs, and a body. Mold them together to look like a person.

11. Warm the green taffy and roll it flat. Cut out the shape of a dress. Wrap the dress around the pink body. Mold the bottom part to look like a wavy skirt.

12. When the wings have hardened, gently push them onto the back of the fairy.

13. Warm the yellow taffy and roll it flat. Cut it into thin strips. Wrap these strips around a toothpick to make them curly. Place them on the fairy's head as hair.

14. To display your fairy ring, place the stump in the center and perch your taffy fairy on top. Surround it with the mushrooms.

Makes 1 fairy, 1 stump, and 5 mushrooms

SPACEY TREATS

Look who landed at your party! These spaceship and alien cookie pops will transport you to a delicious dimension.

INGREDIENTS

2 vanilla wafer cookies
edge icing
green food coloring
flood icing
2 green jelly beans
2 large red gumdrops
1 chocolate striped
    shortbread cookie
sugar pearls

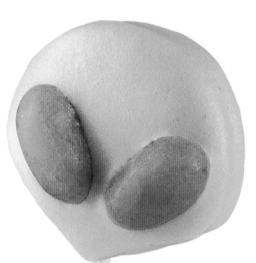

1. Cut the bottom edges of the vanilla wafer cookies so they have a pointed tip.

2. Tint the edge icing green.

3. Scoop a generous blob of edge icing onto the tip of a lollipop stick. Place the stick with frosting on the flat side of one of the cookies. Top it with the other cookie like a sandwich. Let the "cookie pop" harden for about an hour.

4. Tint the flood icing green to match your edge icing.

5. Dip the cookie pop into the green flood icing. Twirl it back and forth and tap the stick on the side of the bowl so the extra frosting drips off.

6. Place the pop flat on a cooling rack with wax paper below to catch extra drips. While the icing is still wet, place on two jelly beans to look like eyes. Let it sit for an hour or more to harden.

7. Thread a gumdrop upside down on a lollipop stick. Next, place the striped cookie upside down. Finally, add another gumdrop on top to hold the cookie on.

8. Pipe green edge icing around the cookie's top edge. Use tweezers to place sugar pearls along the icing line to look like lights.

Makes 2 spacey treats

> *Tip:*
> To display your treats, cover a block of Styrofoam with colorful paper. Then poke your pops in the foam so they stand up.

CURLED UP
COZY CAT

**Curl up with this cozy kitty cat treat.
And see how sweet your fortune can be!**

INGREDIENTS
edge icing
green and orange food coloring
1 large round sugar cookie
flood icing
1 fortune cookie
1 piece pink taffy
1 pink gum ball
2 chocolate sprinkles

1. Take a spoonful of the edge icing and color it green. Divide the rest of the edge icing into two bowls. Color one bowl orange. Leave the other bowl white. Put the icings in piping bags.

2. Pipe a circle of orange edge icing around the sugar cookie.

3. Tint the flood icing orange to match the edge icing.

4. Spoon orange flood icing into the center of the cookie. Use a toothpick to spread it out.

5. Place the fortune cookie on a cooling rack with wax paper beneath. Spoon orange flood icing over the fortune cookie until it is covered. Set both cookies aside to harden for about an hour.

6. Glue the fortune cookie head onto the cookie body with a small dab of icing.

7. Pipe white edge icing on the round cookie to look like a body and tail. Add stripes of white edge icing on the fortune cookie to make face stripes and ear tips.

8. Warm the pink taffy in the microwave for about 5 seconds. Place it in between two pieces of wax paper and roll it flat. Cut out a tiny triangle. With a dab of icing, glue it onto the cat's face as the nose.

9. Cut the rest of the taffy into long, thin strips. Roll them smooth. Wrap them around a gum ball. If you wish, glue the gum ball to the cookie so it looks like the cat has snuggled up with a ball of yarn.

10. With the green edge icing, pipe two small eyes on the fortune cookie. With tweezers, place a chocolate sprinkle vertically within each one.

11. Let the cookie sit for a few hours to completely harden.

Makes 1 cat

FLOWER PLACE CARDS

Flowers are a perfect accent for any table setting. Use these personalized place cards to make every guest feel special.

INGREDIENTS
4 large round sugar cookies
pink, green, and yellow
    food coloring
edge icing
flood icing
sugar pearls
5 chocolate melting wafers

1. Use a cookie cutter to cut a flower shape from one cookie. If the cookie isn't soft enough, place it in the microwave for about 10 seconds before cutting.

2. Use a cookie cutter to cut large leaves from two cookies.

3. Mix up batches of pink and green edge icing. Place the icings in piping bags.

> **Tip:**
> A party host often tries to make all the elements on the table match. Use colors on your place cards that match the napkins, plates, and flowers on your party table.

4. With the pink edge icing, pipe around the outer edge of the flower cookie. Also pipe around the inner edge of the petals, leaving an open area in the center.

5. With the green edge icing, pipe around the edges of the leaf cookies.

6. Mix up batches of pink, yellow, and green flood icing. Spoon the pink icing into the petals of the flower cookie. Spoon the yellow icing into the center of the flower. Spread the icing with a toothpick.

7. With a tweezers, place sugar pearls around the flower's center.

8. Spoon green flood icing on the leaves, using a toothpick to spread.

9. Let the cookies harden for an hour.

10. Place the melting wafers in a small zip-top bag. Leave the bag open and microwave on the defrost setting for 30 seconds. Squeeze the melted candy to one corner. If the wafers are not soft yet, microwave on defrost 30 seconds more. With a kitchen shears, snip off the corner of the bag.

11. Pipe the melted chocolate on the flower, spelling a friend's name.

12. Use edge icing to glue together the three pieces. The flower should be in the center, overlapping the leaves. Let harden for about 15 minutes.

13. Cut the last round cookie in half. Use edge icing to glue half of the cookie onto the back of the flower as a stand.

14. Let the cookies sit for a few hours to completely harden.

Makes 1 place card

monKey AROUND

Sock monkeys are some of the most popular stuffed animals. Bring your toy to the table and have some fun playing with your food.

INGREDIENTS
edge icing
red food coloring
flood icing
oval cookie
1 black licorice whip
1 large round sugar cookie
decorating sugar, any color
1 red licorice whip
2 brown candy-coated
    chocolates
2 candy wafers

1. Divide the edge icing into two small bowls. Add red food coloring to one and leave the other bowl white. Place the icing into piping bags.

2. Divide the flood icing into two small bowls. Add red food coloring to one to match the edge icing. Keep one bowl white.

3. Pipe red edge icing in an oval shape on top of the oval cookie.

4. Spoon the white flood icing over the cookie, being careful not to get any inside the red oval. Then spoon red flood icing inside the oval. Use a toothpick to completely cover.

5. Cut a short length of black licorice whip and place it in the red area for a mouth. Let the cookie harden for 20 minutes.

6. With the white edge icing, pipe a half circle around just over half of the sugar cookie. Then pipe a stripe of frosting where the monkey's forehead would be. Leave an empty space between the half circle and the stripe, and a small space at the top.

7. Spoon white flood icing into the white areas.

8. While the icing is still wet, sprinkle decorating sugar on the white icing. Then put the mouth cookie on the sugar cookie.

9. Pipe stripes with the white edge icing above and below the sugared forehead stripe to fill in the empty areas.

10. Cut a few small strips of red licorice whip and place on top as hair. Place the two candy-coated chocolates as eyes.

11. With the white edge icing, pipe a semi circle on each of the candy wafers. Fill in with the white flood icing. Sprinkle with decorating sugar.

12. With the white edge icing, glue the wafers onto each side of the monkey's head as ears.

13. Let the cookie sit for a few hours to completely harden.

Makes 1 monkey

INGREDIENTS GLOSSARY

chocolate covered
caramels

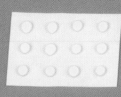

candy buttons

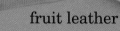

fruit leather

flat, round chocolate
cookies

mini peanut butter
cups

chocolate kisses

taffy

chocolate chews

fruit candy

gingersnap
cookies

mini chocolate chips

chocolate sprinkles

chocolate
sandwich cookies

sour candy strip

black licorice
whip

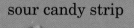

vanilla wafer
cookies

sugared
gumdrops

sugar pearls

striped
shortbread
cookies

decorating
sugar

melting wafers

candy wafers

candy-coated
chocolates

TERMS GLOSSARY

consistency (kuhn-SIS-tuhn-see)—how thick or thin something is

dab (DAB)—a little bit

mold (MOHLD)—to shape something

pipe (PIPE)—to make details by squeezing frosting from a bag

snip (SNIP)—to cut something using small, quick cuts

thread (THRED)—to pass a material through something else

tint (TINT)—to give a slight color

Read more

Blake, Susannah. *Cookies and Cakes.* Make and Eat. New York: PowerKids Press, 2009.

La Penta, Marilyn. *Cool Cookies.* Yummy Tummy Recipes. New York: Bearport Pub., 2012.

Larrew, Brekka Hervey. *Apple Pie Calzones and Other Cookie Recipes.* Fun Food for Cool Cooks. Mankato, Minn.: Capstone Press, 2008.

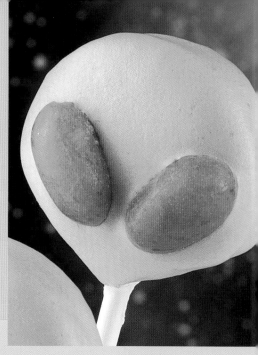

Internet sites

FactHound offers a safe, fun way to find Internet sites related to this book. All of the sites on FactHound have been researched by our staff.

Here's all you do:
Visit *www.facthound.com*
Type in this code: 9781429686198

About the Author

Dana Meachen Rau writes about many topics, including food! When she's not writing, she's being creative in other ways—especially in the kitchen. Sometimes she follows recipes, but other times she experiments with new flavors. And she doesn't need a special occasion to whip up a special dessert for her friends and family in Burlington, Connecticut.

Super-cool stuff! Check out projects, games and lots more at
www.capstonekids.com